"UNLOCKING

DEPTHS: EXPLORING

THE BENEFITS AND

CHALLENGES OF

BOREHOLE WATER

SYSTEMS"

"From Subterranean Reserves to Sustainable Supply: Navigating the Pros and Cons of Borehole Water for Domestic and Agricultural Applications"

BY

DR. CECIL M. HARPER

can the document be copied, scanned, faxed, or retained

without approval from the publisher or creator.

Introduction:

In an ever-changing world where water scarcity and quality are growing concerns, innovative approaches to water supply have become imperative. Borehole water systems have emerged as a promising solution, tapping into the hidden depths of the Earth to secure a vital resource. This comprehensive exploration titled "Unlocking the Depths: Exploring the Benefits and Challenges of Borehole Water Systems" delves into the intricacies of these systems, shedding light on their potential advantages and the complex challenges they present.

Borehole water systems, also known as groundwater wells or artesian wells, involve the extraction of water from beneath the Earth's surface through boreholes drilled deep into the ground. This practice harnesses the natural underground reservoirs that store freshwater, offering a reliable and potentially sustainable water source. The potential benefits are numerous and wide-ranging. Borehole water systems can provide communities with a consistent water supply that is less susceptible to climate fluctuations, making them particularly attractive in regions prone to drought and erratic rainfall patterns.

Furthermore, the utilization of borehole water can alleviate the pressure on surface water sources, reducing the strain on rivers, lakes, and reservoirs that are often overburdened by increasing demand. This aspect becomes crucial in densely populated areas where competition for water resources is intense. Additionally, borehole water systems can empower local communities by granting them greater control over their water supply, enhancing self-sufficiency and resilience in the face of water-related challenges.

However, the journey into the depths of borehole water systems is not without its challenges. The exploration, development, and management of these systems demand a thorough understanding of hydrogeology, engineering, and environmental impacts. Improper drilling techniques or inadequate maintenance can lead to contamination, depleting precious groundwater resources or introducing pollutants into aquifers. Moreover, the overuse of borehole water systems could potentially lead to subsidence or the intrusion of saltwater into freshwater reservoirs, posing serious ecological and infrastructure risks.

As we embark on this comprehensive exploration, we will navigate through the multifaceted landscape of borehole water systems, examining their potential advantages and confronting the intricate challenges they pose. By unraveling the layers of technical, environmental, and social considerations, we seek to gain a holistic understanding of these systems, contributing to informed decision-making and sustainable water management practices in a world where unlocking the depths may hold the key to our water future.

Table of Contents

1.1 Background and Context

The background and context of the exploration into "Unlocking the Depths: Exploring the Benefits and Challenges of Borehole Water Systems" lay the foundation for understanding the significance of this study. As global concerns over water scarcity, quality, and sustainability continue to intensify, the need for innovative and resilient water supply solutions becomes paramount. Borehole water systems, which tap into underground aquifers and reservoirs, offer a potential avenue for securing a stable and dependable water source.

Traditional reliance on surface water bodies, such as rivers, lakes, and reservoirs, has proven to be vulnerable to climatic shifts, pollution, and overextraction. Borehole water systems present an alternative approach that draws water from beneath the Earth's surface, often deep within rock formations. This method capitalizes on the vast reserves of groundwater, which remain relatively insulated from external factors and can serve as a buffer against the uncertainties of changing climate patterns.

In many regions, particularly arid and semi-arid areas, borehole water systems have gained traction as a means of combating water scarcity and ensuring a consistent supply for both domestic and agricultural needs. However, their implementation raises intricate technical, environmental, and societal challenges that must be thoroughly examined and addressed. The exploration of these benefits and challenges aims to contribute to informed decision-making, sustainable practices, and a holistic understanding of the potential role of borehole water systems in shaping the future of water resource management.

By delving into the background and context surrounding borehole water systems, this study endeavors to shed light on the motivations, opportunities, and complexities associated with this innovative approach. By unlocking the depths, we aspire to unearth solutions that harmonize human needs with responsible resource management and environmental stewardship.

1.2 Statement of the Problem

The statement of the problem within the context of "Unlocking the Depths: Exploring the Benefits and Challenges of Borehole Water Systems" identifies and articulates the central issues and concerns that necessitate investigation and analysis in this study.

Water scarcity, deteriorating water quality, and the vulnerability of surface water sources to climate change have prompted the exploration of alternative water supply solutions. Borehole water systems, with their potential to access groundwater reservoirs, offer a promising avenue to address these challenges. However, the successful implementation of borehole water systems is not without its complexities and potential drawbacks.

The primary problem lies in the need to comprehensively assess the benefits and challenges of borehole water systems to ensure their sustainable and effective integration into water resource management strategies. Key issues include:

1. **Technical and Hydrogeological Complexities:**
The intricate subsurface geological and hydrogeological conditions play a pivotal role in determining the feasibility and long-term viability of borehole water systems. A thorough understanding of aquifer characteristics, drilling techniques, and water quality considerations is essential.

2. **Environmental Impacts and Sustainability:**
Borehole water extraction can have ecological consequences, including subsidence, saltwater intrusion, and potential contamination. Balancing water resource development with environmental preservation is a critical challenge.

3. **Community Engagement and Equity:** Ensuring equitable access to borehole water systems and involving local communities in decision-making processes is vital. Disparities in access, potential conflicts, and the empowerment of marginalized groups need to be addressed.

4. **Regulation and Governance:** Establishing effective regulations and governance frameworks for borehole water systems is essential to prevent overexploitation, manage potential conflicts, and safeguard water resources for present and future generations.

5. **Technical Expertise and Capacity Building:** Adequate knowledge, skills, and resources are required for

the proper design, construction, operation, and maintenance of borehole water systems. Building local capacity is crucial for long-term success.

In light of these challenges, a comprehensive analysis is needed to explore both the advantages and potential pitfalls of borehole water systems. This study aims to provide insights, recommendations, and a holistic perspective that can inform policy, decision-making, and sustainable water management practices in various geographical and socio-economic contexts.

1.3 Objectives of the Study

The objectives of the study "Unlocking the Depths: Exploring the Benefits and Challenges of Borehole Water Systems" are outlined as follows:

1. **To Evaluate the Feasibility and Viability of Borehole Water Systems:** This objective involves a detailed examination of the technical, hydrogeological, and engineering aspects of borehole water systems to assess their practicality and potential for sustainable water supply.

2. **To Assess Environmental Impacts and Sustainability:** The study aims to investigate the potential ecological consequences of borehole water systems, such as subsidence, saltwater intrusion, and groundwater contamination. It seeks to provide insights into mitigating these impacts and ensuring the long-term environmental sustainability of these systems.

3. **To Analyze Socioeconomic and Community Factors:** This objective involves an exploration of the social and economic implications of borehole water

systems, including issues of equity, access, community engagement, and empowerment. The study aims to identify strategies for maximizing benefits and minimizing disparities.

4. **To Examine Regulation and Governance Frameworks:** The study will analyze existing regulatory and governance structures related to borehole water systems. It aims to provide recommendations for effective policies, regulations, and management approaches to ensure responsible and equitable use of groundwater resources.

5. **To Provide Case Studies and Lessons Learned:** Through a collection of case studies from different geographical regions, the study intends to showcase successful implementations, as well as instances of challenges and failures. These case studies will offer valuable insights and lessons for future borehole water system projects.

6. **To Suggest Strategies for Capacity Building and Technical Expertise:** The study aims to recommend approaches for building local capacity and technical expertise in borehole water system planning, design, operation, and maintenance. This includes training programs, knowledge dissemination, and skill development.

7. **To Contribute to Informed Decision-Making:**

Ultimately, the study seeks to provide a comprehensive understanding of the benefits and challenges of borehole water systems. By offering evidence-based insights and recommendations, it aims to assist policymakers, water resource managers, and stakeholders in making informed decisions regarding the integration of borehole water systems into broader water management strategies.

Through these objectives, the study endeavors to facilitate a holistic exploration of borehole water systems, promoting their responsible implementation and contributing to sustainable water resource management practices on a global scale.

2. Borehole Water Systems: An Overview

2.1 Definition and Types of Borehole Water Systems

Borehole water systems refer to a category of groundwater extraction methods that involve drilling deep holes, known as boreholes, into the Earth's subsurface to access and extract water from underground aquifers and reservoirs. These systems are designed to tap into hidden water sources beneath the surface, providing a potential solution for water supply in areas facing challenges such as water scarcity, pollution, or unreliable surface water sources.

Types of Borehole Water Systems:

Borehole water systems encompass a range of techniques and configurations tailored to specific geological, hydrological, and water demand conditions. The following are common types of borehole water systems:

1. **Tube Wells:** Tube wells are one of the simplest types of borehole water systems. They typically consist of a perforated pipe or casing inserted into a borehole to

allow water to flow into the well. A pump is used to lift water from the well to the surface.

2. **Dug Wells:** Dug wells involve excavating a hole in the ground until water is reached. The well is often lined with stones, bricks, or other materials to prevent collapse. Dug wells are more common in areas with shallow groundwater tables.

3. **Driven Wells:** Driven wells, also known as sand-point wells, are created by driving a narrow pipe into the ground using a driving point attached to the pipe's lower end. These wells are suitable for shallow aquifers and are relatively easy to install.

4. **Jetted Wells:** Jetted wells are formed by injecting high-pressure water or air into the ground through a small-diameter pipe. The process loosens the soil or sediments, creating a cavity for water to collect. Jetted wells are often used in loose or unconsolidated soils.

5. **Drilled Wells:** Drilled wells are created by rotary drilling methods, typically using a drilling rig. These wells can reach significant depths and are capable of accessing deeper aquifers. They are commonly used in areas with complex geology.

6. **Artesian Wells:** Artesian wells tap into confined aquifers where water is under pressure due to the natural geological structure. When the well is drilled, the pressurized water rises to the surface without the need for pumping.

7. **Pump Types:** Borehole water systems can employ various types of pumps, such as submersible pumps, hand pumps, or solar-powered pumps, to lift water from the well and distribute it for various uses.

Each type of borehole water system has its advantages and limitations, depending on factors like aquifer depth, geological conditions, water demand, and available resources. The selection of the appropriate type of borehole water system is crucial to ensure efficient and sustainable water extraction while minimizing potential environmental and technical challenges.

2.2 How Borehole Water Systems Work

Borehole water systems work by tapping into underground aquifers and reservoirs to extract groundwater for various purposes. The process involves several key components and stages:

1. **Drilling:** The first step in creating a borehole water system is drilling a hole into the ground using specialized equipment, such as a drilling rig. The depth of the borehole depends on factors like the depth of the aquifer and the water demand. The borehole is lined with casing to prevent collapse and to protect the well from contamination.

2. **Installation of Well Screen or Casing:** A well screen or casing is placed in the borehole to prevent soil or sediment from entering the well while allowing water to flow in. The design of the screen or casing is important to ensure efficient water intake and to maintain the structural integrity of the well.

3. **Pumping Mechanism:** A pump is used to extract water from the well and lift it to the surface. The type of pump used depends on factors such as the depth of the well, water demand, and power source availability. Common pump types include submersible pumps, hand pumps, or solar-powered pumps.

4. **Water Extraction:** The pump creates a pressure differential that causes water to flow from the aquifer into the well. The extracted groundwater is then lifted to the surface through the pump mechanism.

5. **Water Treatment and Distribution:** Depending on the intended use of the water, treatment may be required to ensure its quality and safety. Water treatment processes can include filtration, disinfection, and chemical treatment. Once treated, the water is distributed for various purposes, such as drinking, irrigation, industrial processes, or other uses.

6. **Monitoring and Maintenance:** Regular monitoring and maintenance of the borehole water system

are essential to ensure its continued functionality and to prevent potential issues. This may involve checking the pump, monitoring water levels, and conducting water quality tests.

It's important to note that the specific design and operation of a borehole water system can vary based on factors such as the geological conditions of the area, the depth and characteristics of the aquifer, and the technical requirements of the system. Proper planning, engineering, and maintenance are crucial to ensure the effective and sustainable operation of borehole water systems while minimizing potential environmental and health risks.

2.3 Importance of Borehole Water Systems in Water Resource Management

Borehole water systems play a significant role in modern water resource management by offering a range of important benefits and contributions:

1. **Diversification of Water Sources:** Borehole water systems provide an additional source of water supply, diversifying the available sources beyond surface water bodies. This diversification helps reduce the dependence on vulnerable surface water sources that can be affected by pollution, climate variability, and overuse.

2. **Reliability and Resilience:** Groundwater accessed through borehole water systems is often more resilient to short-term variations in climate and weather patterns.

Boreholes can provide a consistent and reliable water supply, particularly during times of drought or erratic rainfall.

3. **Mitigating Water Scarcity:** Borehole water systems offer a solution to regions facing water scarcity challenges. They can provide a lifeline for communities and agriculture in areas where surface water sources are limited, allowing for sustainable water access even during dry periods.

4. **Local Community Empowerment:** Borehole water systems can empower local communities by providing them with a direct, reliable water source. This empowerment enhances community resilience and self-

sufficiency, reducing their dependence on external water supplies.

5. **Agricultural Development:** Borehole water systems are crucial for agricultural development, especially in arid and semi-arid regions. They enable irrigation, allowing farmers to cultivate crops and sustain livestock, thereby contributing to food security and rural livelihoods.

6. **Economic Growth and Industry:** Reliable water supply from borehole water systems can support industrial activities, commercial enterprises, and economic growth. Industries that require substantial water resources, such as

manufacturing and mining, can benefit from a stable and consistent water source.

7. **Water Quality Assurance:** Groundwater is generally less susceptible to contamination compared to surface water. Borehole water systems can provide a source of cleaner water, especially when properly managed and protected from potential sources of pollution.

8. **Reduced Pressure on Surface Water Sources:** By utilizing groundwater through borehole water systems, the strain on surface water bodies such as rivers, lakes, and reservoirs can be reduced. This helps maintain the ecological health of these surface water ecosystems.

9. **Emergency Preparedness:** Borehole water systems can serve as crucial backup sources during emergencies, such as natural disasters or infrastructure failures. Their resilience and reliability can ensure a stable water supply during critical times.

10. **Long-Term Sustainability:** When managed sustainably, borehole water systems can provide a long-term and renewable water supply. Careful monitoring, regulation, and responsible use are essential to prevent overextraction and ensure the continued availability of groundwater resources.

In summary, borehole water systems offer a versatile and valuable tool in the toolbox of water resource management. Their ability to provide reliable, resilient, and sustainable water supply makes them essential for addressing water challenges, supporting communities, and promoting overall socio-economic development.

3. Advantages of Borehole Water Systems

3.1 Reliability and Resilience

Reliability and resilience are key attributes that underscore the importance of borehole water systems in water resource management. These qualities contribute significantly to the effectiveness and sustainability of water supply, especially in the face of various challenges:

1. **Consistent Water Supply:** Borehole water systems provide a dependable and consistent water supply, even during periods of drought or fluctuating weather patterns. Groundwater stored in aquifers is less susceptible

to rapid changes in precipitation, making borehole systems a reliable source when surface water availability is compromised.

2. **Climate Resilience:** Groundwater accessed through borehole systems is generally more resilient to the impacts of climate change. As climate patterns become increasingly unpredictable, borehole systems offer a buffer against water scarcity and fluctuations in surface water availability.

3. **Drought Mitigation:** Borehole water systems play a critical role in mitigating the effects of drought. During prolonged dry spells, surface water sources may become

depleted or contaminated, making boreholes an essential lifeline for communities, agriculture, and ecosystems.

4. **Emergency Preparedness:** Borehole water systems enhance emergency preparedness by providing a stable water source during disasters such as earthquakes, floods, or infrastructure failures. Their robustness and self-contained nature make them valuable assets in times of crisis.

5. **Stability for Agriculture:** Agriculture heavily relies on water supply for irrigation. Borehole water systems offer farmers a dependable source of water, reducing vulnerability to rainfall variability and enabling continuous crop production.

6. **Community Resilience:** Borehole water systems empower local communities by ensuring access to water even when external sources are compromised. This enhances community resilience and reduces their vulnerability to water-related challenges.

7. **Reduced Interference:** Borehole water systems are less susceptible to pollution and surface water contaminants. They provide a degree of separation from human activities that may affect surface water quality.

8. **Long-Term Water Security:** Properly managed borehole water systems contribute to long-term water security by tapping into groundwater resources that are

naturally replenished. With sustainable management, these systems can provide a stable supply for generations.

9. **Flexibility and Adaptability:** Borehole systems offer flexibility in sourcing water from different depths within aquifers, allowing adjustment based on changing demand and hydrological conditions.

10. **Ecosystem Support:** Reliable water supply from borehole systems can help maintain vital ecosystems by reducing the pressure on surface water sources, preserving aquatic habitats, and supporting biodiversity.

In conclusion, the reliability and resilience of borehole water systems make them indispensable tools for ensuring consistent water supply, enhancing community well-being, and promoting sustainable water resource management in an increasingly uncertain and changing world.

3.2 Mitigating Water Scarcity and Drought

Mitigating water scarcity and drought is a critical aspect of borehole water systems, as they offer effective strategies for addressing these pressing challenges:

1. **Diversified Water Sources:** Borehole water systems provide an additional, diversified source of water supply beyond surface water. During periods of water scarcity and drought, when surface water bodies may be depleted, boreholes can continue to provide a reliable water source.

2. **Reliable Access:** Groundwater stored in aquifers, accessed through borehole systems, remains relatively insulated from short-term climatic fluctuations. This reliability ensures a steady water supply even when rainfall patterns are erratic or surface water sources are diminished.

3. **Year-Round Availability:** Borehole water systems can operate year-round, regardless of seasonal variations. They offer a consistent water supply for various needs, such as domestic use, agriculture, and industry, reducing the vulnerability of communities and economies to drought-related disruptions.

4. **Drought-Resilient Agriculture:** Borehole water systems enable irrigation for agricultural purposes, making it possible to cultivate crops during dry spells. This supports food production and helps safeguard rural livelihoods against the impacts of drought on crop yields.

5. **Emergency Response:** Borehole water systems serve as emergency water sources during severe droughts. When surface water sources are insufficient to meet demand, boreholes can provide essential water for drinking, sanitation, and hygiene, ensuring public health and well-being.

6. **Community and Livestock Support:** Borehole water systems are crucial for providing communities and livestock with water during drought. They help maintain basic needs and prevent water-related health risks, particularly in areas where surface water becomes scarce or contaminated.

7. **Reduced Dependence on Precipitation:** Borehole water systems lessen the dependence on precipitation for water supply. This is especially beneficial in regions where rainfall is unreliable or insufficient to meet water demands.

8. **Buffer Against Climate Change:** As climate change leads to increased variability in precipitation and temperature, borehole water systems offer a resilient solution by tapping into groundwater reserves that are less susceptible to immediate climate fluctuations.

9. **Protection of Ecosystems:** By reducing the pressure on surface water bodies during drought, borehole water systems contribute to the protection of aquatic ecosystems and the preservation of aquatic habitats, which are crucial for biodiversity.

10. **Stakeholder Resilience:** Borehole water systems contribute to the resilience of various stakeholders, including communities, farmers, businesses, and industries, by ensuring continued access to water resources even in challenging climatic conditions.

In summary, borehole water systems play a vital role in mitigating the adverse impacts of water scarcity and drought. Their ability to provide consistent and reliable water supply during periods of limited surface water availability helps safeguard human well-being, support agricultural activities, and enhance overall community resilience in the face of changing climate patterns.

3.3 Reduction of Pressure on Surface Water Sources

The reduction of pressure on surface water sources is a significant benefit offered by borehole water systems, contributing to sustainable water resource management and ecosystem preservation:

1. **Conservation of Ecosystems:** Borehole water systems help alleviate the strain on surface water bodies such as rivers, lakes, and reservoirs. By reducing the demand for water from these sources, boreholes contribute

to the conservation of aquatic ecosystems, preserving habitat and biodiversity.

2. **Prevention of Overextraction:** Borehole water systems provide an alternative water source that can help prevent the overextraction of water from surface bodies. This safeguards against the depletion of surface water resources, which can lead to ecological imbalances and diminished water availability for both human and environmental needs.

3. **Water Quality Protection:** Lowering the demand on surface water sources can help maintain better water quality. Overuse of surface water can lead to decreased water levels, higher pollutant concentrations, and increased

vulnerability to contamination, negatively affecting both human health and aquatic ecosystems.

4. **Reduced Competition:** In regions where water resources are limited, competition for surface water can lead to conflicts among various water users, including agriculture, industry, and households. Borehole water systems alleviate this competition by providing an additional water source and reducing the pressure on surface water allocation.

5. **Climate Resilience:** Borehole water systems offer a more resilient water supply option during periods of drought or reduced rainfall. This reduces the need to rely solely on surface water, which may be more vulnerable to the impacts of changing climate patterns.

6. **Sustained Water Flows:** By minimizing excessive extraction from surface water sources, boreholes help maintain natural flow regimes in rivers and streams. This is crucial for the health of aquatic ecosystems, supporting fish migration, sediment transport, and nutrient cycling.

7. **Enhanced Water Security:** Reducing the dependence on surface water sources through borehole systems enhances overall water security. Communities and industries have a more stable supply, especially during times of surface water scarcity or contamination events.

8. **Long-Term Resource Management:** By responsibly managing groundwater extraction through borehole water systems, water managers can ensure the sustainable use of both surface and groundwater resources, supporting long-term resource management goals.

9. **Preservation of Recreation and Aesthetics:** Surface water bodies often serve as recreational and aesthetic spaces. By lessening the pressure on these water bodies, borehole water systems contribute to the preservation of these valuable cultural and recreational resources.

10. **Overall Environmental Balance:** Borehole water systems promote a balanced approach to water

resource management, allowing for the coexistence of human water needs and the ecological well-being of surface water ecosystems.

In conclusion, the reduction of pressure on surface water sources achieved through borehole water systems is instrumental in maintaining ecological integrity, ensuring equitable water allocation, and fostering long-term sustainability in water resource management.

3.4 Empowerment of Local Communities

The empowerment of local communities through borehole water systems has transformative impacts, enhancing their self-reliance, well-being, and overall development:

1. **Direct Access to Water:** Borehole water systems provide local communities with direct access to a reliable and sustainable water source. This empowers them to meet their daily water needs for drinking, sanitation, hygiene, and domestic use without dependency on external water supplies.

2. **Community Engagement:** The involvement of local communities in the planning, implementation, and management of borehole water systems fosters a sense of ownership and responsibility. This engagement strengthens community cohesion, decision-making, and active participation in water resource management.

3. **Enhanced Livelihoods:** Borehole water systems support various livelihood activities, particularly in rural areas. Reliable water access allows communities to engage in agriculture, livestock rearing, and small-scale enterprises, contributing to economic growth and poverty reduction.

4. **Health and Well-Being:** Clean and accessible water from borehole systems improves public health by reducing waterborne diseases. Communities benefit from improved hygiene practices and reduced exposure to contaminants, leading to better overall health and well-being.

5. **Time and Labor Savings:** Borehole water systems alleviate the burden of fetching water, especially for women and children who often bear the responsibility. This frees up valuable time and energy for other productive activities, education, and community engagement.

6. **Empowerment of Women:** Borehole water systems can have a particularly positive impact on women, as they are often primary caregivers responsible for water collection. Access to nearby boreholes reduces the time and physical strain of water fetching, enabling women to engage in income-generating activities and education.

7. **Resilience to Water Scarcity:** Communities with borehole access are more resilient during water scarcity and drought. The reliability of borehole systems ensures water availability even when surface water sources are compromised.

8. **Education Opportunities:** With reduced water collection burdens, children, especially girls, have improved access to education. Borehole water systems contribute to increased school attendance and improved educational outcomes.

9. **Cultural and Social Empowerment:** Reliable water access enhances cultural practices, communal gatherings, and social interactions within the community. Boreholes can serve as central points for community activities, contributing to cultural preservation and cohesion.

10. **Capacity Building:** The planning, maintenance, and management of borehole water systems often involve training and capacity-building initiatives. This empowers community members with valuable technical skills, enabling them to take an active role in sustaining their water supply.

11. **Community Resilience:** By providing local communities with a self-sufficient water source, borehole systems enhance their resilience to external water-related challenges, such as pollution, water price fluctuations, and supply interruptions.

12. **Partnership and Collaboration:** Borehole projects can foster collaboration between communities,

local governments, NGOs, and other stakeholders. This collective effort strengthens local governance and facilitates the sharing of knowledge and resources.

In essence, the empowerment of local communities through borehole water systems extends beyond mere water access. It transforms lives, fosters development, and empowers individuals to create lasting positive change within their communities.

4. Challenges of Borehole Water Systems

4.1 Hydrogeological Considerations and Exploration

Hydrogeological considerations and exploration are fundamental to the successful implementation of borehole water systems. These aspects involve a detailed understanding of the subsurface characteristics and the hydrological behavior of groundwater. Here's an overview:

1. **Aquifer Characterization:** Hydrogeological exploration begins with the characterization of aquifers – underground geological formations that contain and transmit water. This involves studying their depth, thickness, porosity, permeability, and hydraulic conductivity. Such data help determine the potential yield of water that can be extracted from the aquifer.

2. **Groundwater Flow Patterns:** Understanding the flow patterns of groundwater is crucial. Hydrogeologists analyze factors influencing groundwater movement, such as hydraulic gradients, recharge areas, and discharge zones.

This knowledge guides the placement of boreholes to optimize water extraction.

3. **Geological and Hydrogeological Mapping:** Geological and hydrogeological mapping helps identify the rock formations and sediment layers that store and transmit groundwater. It assists in locating suitable drilling sites and predicting potential challenges during drilling.

4. **Hydrological Surveys:** These surveys involve measuring water levels in existing wells and monitoring seasonal fluctuations. Data collected provide insights into aquifer behavior, helping estimate sustainable yield and preventing overextraction.

5. **Geophysical Techniques:** Methods like resistivity surveys, seismic refraction, and ground-penetrating radar are employed to image subsurface structures. These techniques aid in identifying aquifer boundaries, potential contamination zones, and optimal drilling depths.

6. **Pilot Boreholes and Test Pumping:** Pilot boreholes are drilled to assess aquifer properties and water quality. Test pumping involves pumping water from a well at varying rates to measure how the aquifer responds. This helps estimate sustainable pumping rates and potential impacts on nearby wells.

7. **Water Quality Analysis:** Hydrogeological exploration includes water quality testing to ensure that extracted groundwater meets drinking water standards. Analysis involves assessing factors like pH, salinity, mineral content, and potential contaminants.

8. **Environmental Impact Assessment:** Exploration also considers potential environmental impacts. It assesses risks of aquifer contamination, subsidence, and saltwater intrusion, which could result from improper drilling or excessive pumping.

9. **Hydrogeological Modeling:** Advanced computer modeling simulates groundwater flow and interactions. This aids in predicting aquifer responses to pumping and provides insights into long-term sustainability.

10. **Permitting and Regulation:** Hydrogeological considerations extend to regulatory requirements. Permits may be necessary to drill boreholes, and compliance with groundwater protection regulations is essential.

11. **Community Engagement:** Engaging local communities is vital to understand their water needs and concerns. Their traditional knowledge can provide insights into groundwater behavior and influence borehole placement.

In essence, hydrogeological considerations and exploration ensure that borehole water systems are designed and implemented based on a thorough understanding of the subsurface hydrology. This knowledge mitigates risks, optimizes water extraction, and supports sustainable water management practices.

4.2 Engineering and Technical Challenges

Implementing borehole water systems presents several engineering and technical challenges that require careful consideration and expertise. These challenges span from borehole design to system operation and maintenance:

1. **Borehole Design and Construction:** Designing boreholes that are structurally sound, properly lined, and adequately sealed is crucial. Inadequate design can lead to collapsing boreholes, water contamination, or the entry of unwanted materials.

2. **Aquifer Compatibility:** Ensuring compatibility between the borehole and the aquifer is vital. If the borehole is not properly suited to the hydrogeological conditions, it may not yield sufficient water, or the water quality may be compromised.

3. **Pump Selection and Sizing:** Selecting the appropriate pump type and size is essential for efficient water extraction. An improper pump can lead to energy inefficiency, premature pump failure, or inadequate water supply.

4. **Pumping Rate and Drawdown Management:** Over-pumping from boreholes can cause a drop in the water table, affecting neighboring wells and ecosystems.

Proper management of pumping rates and monitoring drawdown is critical to prevent resource depletion.

5. **Water Quality Monitoring and Treatment:** Ensuring water quality is a challenge. Groundwater can carry minerals, contaminants, or pathogens that require treatment to meet safe drinking water standards.

6. **Energy Source:** Selecting a suitable and reliable energy source for pumping operations is crucial. Depending on the location, solar, grid electricity, or other sources may be chosen.

7. **System Resilience and Redundancy:** Developing resilient borehole water systems with backup power solutions and redundancy mechanisms is important to ensure continuous water supply, especially during power outages.

8. **Maintenance and Repairs:** Regular maintenance of pumps, pipes, and associated equipment is essential for system longevity. Lack of maintenance can lead to equipment failure and interruption of water supply.

9. **Capacity Building:** Training local technicians and communities to operate and maintain borehole water systems is necessary for long-term sustainability. Adequate knowledge transfer ensures that systems continue to function effectively.

10. **Budget Constraints:** Budget limitations can impact the quality of components and construction, potentially leading to suboptimal system performance or premature failures.

11. **Community Engagement and Acceptance:** Gaining community buy-in and addressing their needs and concerns is critical. Lack of acceptance can lead to underutilization or improper maintenance of the systems.

12. **Regulatory Compliance:** Navigating regulatory frameworks, obtaining permits, and adhering to environmental regulations are crucial for responsible implementation.

Addressing these engineering and technical challenges requires multidisciplinary expertise, stakeholder collaboration, and a thorough understanding of the local hydrogeological and socio-economic context. Proper planning, design, and implementation are essential to ensure the effective and sustainable operation of borehole water systems.

4.3 Environmental Impacts and Sustainability

Environmental impacts and sustainability considerations are paramount when implementing borehole water systems, as they help ensure responsible water resource management and minimize negative effects on ecosystems and the environment. Key aspects include:

1. **Groundwater Depletion:** Over-pumping from boreholes can lead to groundwater depletion, causing aquifer levels to drop and potentially impacting the long-term sustainability of the water source.

2. **Ecological Disruption:** Excessive groundwater extraction can affect ecosystems dependent on groundwater, such as wetlands, rivers, and vegetation. Reduced groundwater levels may alter habitat availability and disrupt ecological processes.

3. **Saltwater Intrusion:** In coastal areas, excessive groundwater extraction can induce saltwater intrusion into freshwater aquifers, rendering water unsuitable for consumption or irrigation.

4. **Subsidence:** Over-pumping can lead to land subsidence as underground voids collapse. This phenomenon may result in ground surface sinking and infrastructure damage.

5. **Contamination Risk:** Poorly designed or maintained boreholes can introduce contaminants into the aquifer or draw in pollutants from surrounding areas, compromising water quality.

6. **Ecosystem Hotspots:** Boreholes that provide constant water supply can attract wildlife, potentially concentrating animal activity in specific areas, impacting biodiversity, and leading to conflicts with humans.

7. **Changes in Surface Water Flows:** Excessive groundwater extraction can reduce baseflow to rivers and streams, affecting aquatic habitats, sediment transport, and nutrient cycling.

8. **Water-Related Land Use Changes:** The availability of borehole water may lead to changes in land use, such as increased agriculture or urban development, which can alter the natural landscape and ecosystem dynamics.

9. **Energy Consumption:** Borehole water systems require energy for pumping. High energy consumption, especially from non-renewable sources, can contribute to carbon emissions and climate change.

To ensure environmental sustainability, the following approaches are recommended:

1. **Aquifer Sustainability Assessment:** Conduct comprehensive aquifer studies to determine sustainable pumping rates that balance water withdrawal with natural recharge rates.

2. **Monitoring and Regulation:** Implement monitoring programs to track groundwater levels, quality, and environmental indicators. Develop and enforce regulations to prevent over-extraction and contamination.

3. **Recharge Enhancement:** Explore methods to enhance aquifer recharge, such as managed aquifer

recharge projects, rainwater harvesting, and improved land management practices.

4. **Mitigation Measures:** Implement measures to mitigate impacts, such as managed drawdown of wells to reduce subsidence risks or controlling pumping during critical periods for ecosystems.

5. **Ecosystem-Friendly Designs:** Incorporate features that benefit ecosystems, such as constructed wetlands or artificial recharge systems, alongside borehole water systems.

6. **Community Education:** Raise awareness among users about sustainable water use, proper waste disposal, and the importance of maintaining groundwater quality.

7. **Renewable Energy Integration:** Whenever possible, integrate renewable energy sources like solar power to reduce the carbon footprint of pumping operations.

8. **Adaptive Management:** Continuously assess the performance of borehole water systems and adapt management practices based on changing hydrogeological and environmental conditions.

By prioritizing environmental sustainability in the planning, implementation, and management of borehole water systems, communities can ensure long-term access to water resources while safeguarding ecosystems and minimizing negative impacts.

4.4 Risk of Overextraction and Resource Depletion

The risk of overextraction and resource depletion is a significant concern associated with borehole water systems, particularly when groundwater is not managed sustainably. Overextraction can lead to a range of negative consequences:

1. **Groundwater Depletion:** Continued over-pumping can lead to the lowering of groundwater levels

within aquifers, depleting the stored water volume and reducing the aquifer's ability to naturally recharge.

2. **Decreased Well Yield:** Overextraction can lead to decreased well yield over time as the water table drops, resulting in reduced water availability for users who depend on the borehole.

3. **Well Drying and Pump Burnout:** In extreme cases, overextraction can cause wells to run dry, rendering them non-functional. Over-pumping can also lead to pump burnout, damaging pumping equipment due to excessive workload.

4. **Impact on Nearby Wells:** Overextraction from one borehole can impact neighboring wells, causing them to experience drawdown and reduced water availability, especially in densely populated areas.

5. **Subsidence:** Over-pumping can result in land subsidence as the voids in the aquifer collapse. This can lead to infrastructure damage, increased flood risk, and changes in the landscape.

6. **Saltwater Intrusion:** In coastal areas, overextraction can cause saltwater to intrude into freshwater aquifers, rendering the water source saline and unsuitable for consumption or irrigation.

7. **Ecosystem Effects:** Overextraction can harm ecosystems that depend on groundwater, affecting wetlands, springs, and vegetation that rely on a certain water table level.

To mitigate the risk of overextraction and resource depletion:

1. **Aquifer Assessments:** Conduct thorough hydrogeological assessments to understand the aquifer's characteristics, natural recharge rates, and sustainable yield to determine safe extraction limits.

2. **Monitoring Programs:** Establish regular monitoring of groundwater levels and pump rates to track trends and potential declining water levels.

3. **Withdrawal Limits:** Implement regulations and guidelines that set withdrawal limits based on the aquifer's safe yield to prevent excessive pumping.

4. **Adaptive Management:** Continuously adjust pumping rates based on aquifer response and environmental changes, employing adaptive management strategies.

5. **Water Use Efficiency:** Promote water use efficiency practices among borehole users, including conservation measures, leak detection, and water-saving technologies.

6. **Aquifer Recharge:** Implement managed aquifer recharge techniques to replenish groundwater during wet periods and help maintain aquifer levels.

7. **Community Education:** Educate users about the importance of sustainable groundwater management and the potential consequences of overextraction.

8. **Integrated Water Management:** Integrate borehole water systems into broader water resource management plans that consider surface water, groundwater, and other water sources holistically.

By addressing the risks associated with overextraction and resource depletion, borehole water systems can be managed in a way that ensures long-term availability, environmental protection, and the sustainable use of groundwater resources.

5. Hydrogeological Exploration and Assessment

5.1 Groundwater Mapping and Aquifer Characterization

Groundwater mapping and aquifer characterization are essential processes that provide valuable insights into the distribution, properties, and behavior of groundwater resources. These activities play a crucial role in effectively managing and utilizing borehole water systems. Here's an overview of groundwater mapping and aquifer characterization:

Groundwater Mapping:

Groundwater mapping involves the spatial representation of groundwater resources and their variations within a specific area. This process provides a comprehensive understanding of the distribution of groundwater levels, flow patterns, and potential sources of recharge and discharge. Groundwater maps are created using various techniques and data sources:

1. **Topographic Maps:** These maps show elevation contours and can help identify potential groundwater recharge areas based on landforms and slopes.

2. **Geological Maps:** Geological maps illustrate subsurface rock formations and structures, aiding in identifying potential aquifer locations and characteristics.

3. **Hydrogeological Maps:** These maps depict the hydrogeological properties of the subsurface, including aquifer types, thickness, and groundwater flow directions.

4. **Water Level Maps:** These maps display groundwater level contours, indicating areas of high and low water tables. They provide insights into groundwater flow patterns and recharge zones.

5. **Isotope Analysis:** Isotopic studies help trace the origin and movement of groundwater by analyzing the stable isotopes of water molecules.

6. **Geophysical Surveys:** Techniques like resistivity surveys and ground-penetrating radar can provide subsurface information to map groundwater-bearing formations.

Aquifer Characterization:

Aquifer characterization involves detailed assessment of the properties and behavior of aquifers, which are geological formations that contain and transmit groundwater. This information is crucial for designing and operating borehole water systems:

1. **Hydraulic Properties:** Aquifer properties such as porosity (void spaces within rocks) and permeability (ability to transmit water) are determined through laboratory tests and field measurements.

2. **Transmissivity and Specific Yield:** These parameters help quantify the ability of an aquifer to transmit water and its storage capacity, respectively.

3. **Hydrogeological Testing:** Pump tests and slug tests provide data on aquifer response to pumping or water

level changes, aiding in estimating sustainable pumping rates.

4. **Groundwater Chemistry:** Analyzing groundwater chemistry provides insights into water quality, mineral content, and potential contaminants.

5. **Aquifer Boundaries:** Identifying aquifer boundaries and potential barriers helps understand aquifer extent and potential interactions with neighboring aquifers.

6. **Recharge and Discharge Areas:** Aquifer characterization helps identify areas where groundwater is recharged (infiltrates) and discharged (flows to the surface or into streams).

7. **Aquifer Vulnerability:** Assessing aquifer vulnerability involves evaluating its susceptibility to contamination based on factors like soil type, land use, and hydrogeological conditions.

By conducting thorough groundwater mapping and aquifer characterization, water resource managers, hydrogeologists, and engineers can make informed decisions about borehole siting, sustainable pumping rates, and water quality considerations, ensuring the responsible and efficient use of groundwater resources.

5.2 Drilling Techniques and Site Selection

Drilling techniques and site selection are critical components in the successful implementation of borehole water systems. Properly chosen drilling methods and well locations contribute to the efficiency, reliability, and sustainability of these systems. Here's an overview:

Drilling Techniques:

Different drilling techniques are used based on factors such as the geological conditions, desired well depth, and available equipment. Common drilling methods include:

1. **Rotary Drilling:** This technique involves using a rotating drill bit to cut through rock formations. It is suitable for hard rock and can achieve greater depths.

2. **Percussion Drilling:** Percussion drilling uses repetitive impacts to break rocks and create boreholes. It is

effective in softer formations and can be used for shallower wells.

3. **Auger Drilling:** Auger drilling employs a rotating helical screw to remove soil and sediments. It's suitable for unconsolidated materials and is often used for shallower wells.

4. **Cable Tool Drilling:** Also known as "spudding," cable tool drilling raises and drops a heavy drill bit repeatedly to break rocks. It is often used for shallow wells in hard rock.

5. **Directional Drilling:** This method involves drilling at an angle or horizontally to access specific

geological formations. It's used when vertical drilling is not feasible or when targeting specific zones.

6. **Hydraulic Rotary Drilling:** This technique uses high-pressure water to rotate the drill bit and simultaneously flush cuttings to the surface.

7. **Sonic Drilling:** Sonic drilling employs high-frequency vibrations to break rocks and remove cuttings, allowing for faster drilling and reduced sample contamination.

Site Selection:

Choosing the right location for boreholes is crucial to ensure optimal water yield, water quality, and longevity of the system. Consider the following factors during site selection:

1. **Hydrogeological Conditions:** Understand the local hydrogeology, including aquifer type, depth, and recharge patterns, to identify areas with suitable groundwater resources.

2. **Topography:** Select sites in areas with proper topography to facilitate groundwater flow and avoid potential contamination sources.

3. **Land Use:** Avoid areas with heavy industrial or agricultural activities that could lead to groundwater contamination.

4. **Proximity to Pollution Sources:** Ensure boreholes are situated a safe distance from potential pollution sources, such as septic systems, waste disposal sites, or chemical storage facilities.

5. **Accessibility:** Consider ease of access for drilling equipment, maintenance, and future repairs.

6. **Community Input:** Involve local communities in the site selection process to ensure that their water needs, concerns, and traditional knowledge are taken into account.

7. **Legal and Regulatory Requirements:** Adhere to local regulations and obtain necessary permits for drilling and well construction.

8. **Safety Considerations:** Prioritize safety during drilling by assessing potential hazards and implementing proper safety measures.

9. **Geological Survey:** Conduct a geological survey to understand subsurface conditions and identify potential drilling challenges.

10. **Future Expansion:** Consider the potential for future boreholes or system expansion to meet growing water demands.

By carefully selecting suitable drilling techniques and well locations, borehole water systems can be designed to maximize water availability, quality, and sustainability while minimizing risks and challenges.

5.3 Water Quality Assessment and Monitoring

Water quality assessment and monitoring are crucial components of borehole water systems to ensure the safety, reliability, and sustainability of the water supply. Regular evaluation of water quality helps identify any potential contaminants or changes in water composition. Here's an overview of water quality assessment and monitoring:

Water Quality Assessment:

Water quality assessment involves analyzing various physical, chemical, and biological parameters to determine if the water meets established safety and health standards. Key aspects of water quality assessment include:

1. **Physical Parameters:** These include temperature, pH (acidity/alkalinity), turbidity (clarity), and color. Deviations from acceptable ranges may indicate water quality issues.

2. **Chemical Parameters:** Testing for minerals, nutrients, heavy metals, and pollutants is essential. Parameters such as nitrate, fluoride, arsenic, lead, and chloride are commonly assessed.

3. **Biological Parameters:** Microbiological testing involves detecting the presence of bacteria, viruses, and other pathogens. Coliform bacteria, E. coli, and total microbial counts are frequently examined.

4. **Dissolved Oxygen (DO):** DO levels indicate the oxygen content in water, which is critical for supporting aquatic life.

5. **Total Dissolved Solids (TDS):** TDS measurement provides insights into the concentration of dissolved minerals in water.

6. **Water Hardness:** Hardness refers to the concentration of calcium and magnesium ions and can impact the taste and usability of water.

7. **Chlorine Residual:** Chlorine levels are assessed to ensure disinfection effectiveness and to monitor residual chlorine concentrations.

8. **Other Contaminants:** Depending on local conditions, additional parameters like pesticides, volatile organic compounds (VOCs), and emerging contaminants may also be tested.

****Water Quality Monitoring:****

Continuous or periodic water quality monitoring involves regular testing of borehole water to track changes over time and detect any emerging issues. Key aspects of water quality monitoring include:

1. **Sampling Frequency:** Establish a schedule for water sampling and testing based on factors such as usage volume, water source vulnerability, and regulatory requirements.

2. **Sample Collection:** Collect samples following proper protocols to ensure representative and accurate results. Samples may be collected at the source or at designated points in the distribution system.

3. **Laboratory Analysis:** Send collected samples to certified laboratories for analysis. Ensure that the chosen laboratory is capable of conducting the required tests.

4. **Data Interpretation:** Interpret the laboratory results and compare them to relevant water quality standards or guidelines. Identify any deviations and take appropriate actions if necessary.

5. **Alert Systems:** Implement alert systems that trigger notifications when specific water quality parameters exceed acceptable limits, enabling rapid response.

6. **Documentation:** Maintain detailed records of water quality data, testing procedures, and any corrective

actions taken. Documentation is important for accountability and decision-making.

7. **Community Engagement:** Involve the community in the monitoring process, share water quality information, and encourage their active participation in maintaining safe water.

By regularly assessing and monitoring water quality, borehole water systems can promptly address potential issues, ensure compliance with health standards, and provide safe and reliable water to communities.

6. Engineering Aspects of Borehole Water Systems

6.1 Borehole Design and Construction

Borehole design and construction are crucial stages in the development of borehole water systems. A well-designed and properly constructed borehole ensures efficient water extraction, minimizes potential risks, and contributes to the long-term sustainability of the system. Here's an overview of borehole design and construction:

Borehole Design:

Borehole design involves determining the specifications and characteristics of the borehole, taking into account factors such as hydrogeological conditions, intended water use, and local regulations. Key aspects of borehole design include:

1. **Borehole Depth:** Determine the appropriate depth based on the target aquifer's location, yield, and water

quality. Ensure that the borehole extends into the productive zone of the aquifer.

2. **Casing and Screen Selection:** Choose suitable casing materials (such as PVC or steel) and screen designs to prevent borehole collapse, control sediment entry, and facilitate water entry. The screen allows water to flow into the borehole while filtering out particles.

3. **Borehole Diameter:** Select the borehole diameter based on the well pump size and future maintenance needs. A larger diameter may be required for well development and cleaning.

4. **Grouting:** Proper grouting (sealing the annular space between the borehole wall and casing) prevents contamination and ensures structural integrity. Grout material and installation methods should be chosen carefully.

5. **Wellhead Configuration:** Design the wellhead to protect the borehole from surface contaminants, debris, and unauthorized access. It should include features such as a secure cover, sanitary seal, and proper drainage.

6. **Borehole Development:** Plan for borehole development techniques, such as surging, jetting, or airlifting, to remove drilling fluids and fine materials from the borehole.

Borehole Construction:

Borehole construction involves physically drilling, casing, and completing the borehole according to the designed specifications. Proper construction techniques are critical to ensure borehole integrity and water quality. Key aspects of borehole construction include:

1. **Site Preparation:** Clear the drilling site and ensure accessibility for drilling equipment. Address safety considerations and implement proper safeguards.

2. **Drilling:** Use appropriate drilling techniques based on geological conditions. Drill through overburden and

into the target aquifer, monitoring drilling progress and collecting samples as needed.

3. **Casing Installation:** Insert casing into the borehole as drilling progresses. The casing should extend from the surface down to the productive aquifer, preventing borehole collapse and contamination.

4. **Grouting:** After casing installation, grout the annular space between the casing and borehole wall using approved grout materials. Grouting seals off potential pathways for contaminants to enter the borehole.

5. **Well Development:** Develop the borehole using techniques such as surging, jetting, or pumping to remove

drilling mud, sediment, and fine materials, and to enhance water flow from the aquifer.

6. **Screen Installation:** Install the well screen in the productive aquifer section of the borehole. The screen allows water to enter while minimizing sediment inflow.

7. **Wellhead Installation:** Assemble and install the wellhead equipment, including the casing head, sanitary seal, and protective cover.

8. **Testing and Verification:** Conduct tests to ensure proper well construction, such as yield tests to assess water flow rates, and water quality tests to verify the absence of contaminants.

9. **Documentation:** Maintain accurate records of borehole construction activities, materials used, and test results. Proper documentation is essential for future maintenance and compliance.

Proper borehole design and construction are essential for the functionality, safety, and longevity of borehole water systems. Adhering to best practices and regulations helps ensure that the borehole effectively taps into groundwater resources while safeguarding water quality and environmental integrity.

6.2 Pumping and Distribution Systems

Pumping and distribution systems are integral components of borehole water systems that enable the extraction, transportation, and delivery of groundwater to end-users. These systems play a crucial role in ensuring reliable access to clean and safe water. Here's an overview of pumping and distribution systems:

Pumping Systems:

Pumping systems are responsible for extracting groundwater from the borehole and delivering it to the surface for further treatment and distribution. Key aspects of pumping systems include:

1. **Well Pump Selection:** Choose an appropriate pump type (submersible, jet, hand pump, etc.) based on

factors such as borehole depth, water yield, and energy source availability.

2. **Pump Sizing:** Size the pump correctly to match the borehole's capacity and the anticipated water demand. Oversized or undersized pumps can lead to inefficiency or system failure.

3. **Energy Source:** Determine the energy source for pumping operations. This could be electricity from the grid, solar power, wind power, or a combination of sources based on site conditions.

4. **Pump Operation:** Set up controls and automation for pump operation, including starting and stopping based on water level sensors or timers.

5. **Backup Power:** Consider backup power solutions, such as generators or battery storage, to ensure continuous water supply during power outages.

6. **Maintenance and Repairs:** Develop a maintenance schedule for pumps and associated equipment to prevent breakdowns and ensure reliable operation.

Distribution Systems:

Distribution systems ensure that water is transported from the source to consumers, whether households, businesses, or other users. Key aspects of distribution systems include:

1. **Piping Network:** Design a piping network that efficiently transports water to various distribution points while minimizing pressure losses and ensuring adequate flow rates.

2. **Distribution Points:** Establish distribution points, such as taps, standpipes, or water kiosks, at strategic locations to ensure convenient access for users.

3. **Pressure Regulation:** Install pressure-reducing valves or other devices to regulate water pressure, prevent pipe bursts, and ensure consistent flow.

4. **Water Treatment:** Depending on water quality, consider adding treatment facilities such as chlorination, filtration, or disinfection before distribution.

5. **Storage Facilities:** Include storage tanks to buffer water supply and manage peak demand periods. Tanks also provide a reserve during pump maintenance or power outages.

6. **Hygiene and Sanitation:** Ensure distribution points are designed to prevent contamination and maintain hygiene standards.

7. **Community Participation:** Involve the community in the design and planning of distribution systems to ensure their needs are met and to promote ownership.

8. **Water Metering:** Install water meters at distribution points to monitor consumption, promote responsible use, and aid in revenue collection if applicable.

9. **Education and Outreach:** Provide users with information on proper water use, maintenance of distribution points, and hygiene practices.

Monitoring and Management:

Implement monitoring and management strategies to ensure the efficient operation of pumping and distribution systems:

1. **Remote Monitoring:** Use sensors and remote monitoring technology to track water levels, pump performance, and system status in real time.

2. **Data Collection:** Gather data on water demand, distribution losses, and system performance to inform decision-making and future planning.

3. **System Optimization:** Continuously analyze data to identify opportunities for system optimization, energy efficiency improvements, and leakage reduction.

4. **Emergency Response:** Develop contingency plans for system failures, supply interruptions, or other emergencies to ensure a rapid and effective response.

Effective pumping and distribution systems are essential for providing consistent, safe, and reliable water access to communities. By carefully designing, implementing, and maintaining these systems, borehole water systems can meet the water needs of users while ensuring efficient resource utilization.

6.3 Maintenance and Rehabilitation

Maintenance and rehabilitation are critical aspects of borehole water systems to ensure their long-term functionality, efficiency, and sustainability. Regular maintenance activities and timely rehabilitation efforts help prevent system failures, extend the lifespan of components, and maintain water quality. Here's an overview of maintenance and rehabilitation practices:

Maintenance Practices:

Regular maintenance involves routine tasks aimed at preserving the operational efficiency of the borehole water system. Key maintenance practices include:

1. **Scheduled Inspections:** Conduct regular visual inspections of the borehole, pump, wellhead, and distribution points to identify signs of wear, damage, or leaks.

2. **Pump Maintenance:** Service the pump, motor, and associated electrical components according to manufacturer recommendations. Clean, lubricate, and replace worn parts as needed.

3. **Cleaning and Disinfection:** Regularly clean and disinfect storage tanks, distribution points, and wellheads to prevent the buildup of sediment, biofilm, and microbial contamination.

4. **Pressure Testing:** Periodically test and adjust pressure settings in the distribution system to ensure optimal water flow and pressure regulation.

5. **Water Quality Testing:** Conduct routine water quality testing to monitor changes in water chemistry and identify any contamination issues.

6. **Leak Detection:** Implement leak detection programs to identify and repair leaks in the distribution network promptly, reducing water losses.

7. **Energy Efficiency:** Optimize energy use by maintaining pumps, motors, and other electrical components for peak efficiency.

8. **Training:** Train local operators and technicians to perform routine maintenance tasks and address minor repairs.

9. **Community Engagement:** Engage the community in maintaining the borehole water system and promote a sense of ownership and responsibility.

Rehabilitation and Repairs:

Over time, components of the borehole water system may deteriorate or malfunction. Rehabilitation involves more extensive efforts to restore the system's functionality. Key rehabilitation and repair practices include:

1. **Borehole Cleaning:** If sediment buildup or clogging occurs, professional borehole cleaning using techniques such as airlifting or surging may be necessary.

2. **Well Development:** Perform well development techniques to improve water flow and remove fine materials that may have entered the borehole.

3. **Casing and Grouting Repair:** Repair damaged or corroded casing and grout to maintain borehole integrity and prevent contamination.

4. **Pump Replacement:** When pumps reach the end of their lifespan or fail, replace them with appropriate-sized, efficient pumps.

5. **Infrastructure Upgrades:** Upgrade distribution infrastructure, storage tanks, and distribution points as needed to meet growing demand and improve system performance.

6. **Water Treatment Enhancements:** Upgrade or modify water treatment facilities to address changing water quality challenges.

7. **Pipeline Rehabilitation:** Repair or replace damaged pipes, fittings, and valves in the distribution network to reduce water losses and maintain pressure.

8. **Community Collaboration:** Engage the community in identifying rehabilitation needs, prioritizing repairs, and participating in rehabilitation efforts.

Lifecycle Planning and Budgeting:

Develop a lifecycle plan and budget for borehole water systems to ensure adequate funding for maintenance, repairs, and eventual replacements. Consider the estimated lifespan of components and plan for regular system assessments to identify upcoming rehabilitation needs.

By implementing proactive maintenance practices and timely rehabilitation efforts, borehole water systems can operate effectively, provide reliable water supply, and contribute to the well-being of communities over the long term.

7. Environmental Considerations and Sustainability

7.1 Potential Ecological Impacts

Borehole water systems, while providing essential water resources for human use, can have potential ecological impacts that need careful consideration and management. These impacts can affect local ecosystems, biodiversity, and natural habitats. Here are some potential ecological impacts associated with borehole water systems:

1. **Groundwater Depletion:** Excessive groundwater extraction from boreholes can lead to lowered water tables and reduced groundwater flow to streams, wetlands, and rivers. This can disrupt aquatic ecosystems and impact the habitats of plants and animals that depend on groundwater.

2. **Surface Water Discharge:** Borehole water systems that discharge excess water onto the land surface can alter the natural flow patterns of surface water bodies, affecting aquatic habitats and water-dependent organisms.

3. **Wetland and Riparian Zones:** Changes in groundwater levels due to borehole pumping can impact wetlands and riparian zones. Lowered water tables may

lead to the drying out of wetlands, affecting the plants and animals that rely on these habitats.

4. **Ecosystem Hotspots:** Boreholes providing a consistent water source can attract wildlife, leading to increased animal activity around these sites. This concentration of activity can impact local biodiversity and may lead to conflicts between wildlife and humans.

5. **Saltwater Intrusion:** In coastal areas, excessive groundwater extraction can induce saltwater intrusion into freshwater aquifers, affecting coastal ecosystems and reducing the availability of freshwater resources.

6. **Species Displacement:** Altered groundwater flow patterns or water availability can result in changes to plant species composition and distribution, potentially displacing native vegetation and favoring invasive species.

7. **Microbial Communities:** Changes in water levels and flow patterns can influence microbial communities in soil and aquatic habitats, which play critical roles in nutrient cycling and ecosystem health.

8. **Water-Dependent Fauna:** Reduced groundwater availability can impact aquatic and semi-aquatic species such as amphibians, reptiles, and small mammals that rely on groundwater-fed habitats.

9. **Erosion and Sedimentation:** Altered groundwater levels can impact soil moisture, potentially leading to increased erosion and sedimentation in water bodies, affecting aquatic habitats.

10. **Thermal Changes:** Extraction of groundwater may alter temperature patterns in aquifers and surface water bodies, potentially impacting temperature-sensitive aquatic organisms.

To mitigate potential ecological impacts, it's important to:

- **Conduct Environmental Assessments:** Before implementing borehole water systems, conduct thorough environmental assessments to understand the potential impacts on local ecosystems.

- **Monitor and Manage:** Regularly monitor groundwater levels, surface water interactions, and ecological changes in the vicinity of boreholes. Implement management strategies to mitigate adverse effects.

- **Use Sustainable Practices:** Implement sustainable groundwater management practices that consider ecosystem needs and prioritize the long-term health of local habitats.

- **Local Engagement:** Involve local communities, conservation organizations, and environmental experts in the planning, implementation, and monitoring of borehole water systems to ensure that ecological impacts are minimized.

By taking a holistic and environmentally conscious approach to borehole water systems, it is possible to provide essential water resources while minimizing negative ecological consequences.

7.2 Groundwater Contamination and Remediation

Groundwater contamination is a significant concern associated with borehole water systems. Contamination can occur when pollutants from various sources infiltrate the groundwater, potentially impacting the quality of water extracted from boreholes. Effective remediation strategies are essential to address groundwater contamination and ensure safe water supply. Here's an overview of groundwater contamination and remediation:

Sources of Groundwater Contamination:

Groundwater contamination can arise from a variety of sources, including:

1. **Point Source Pollution:** Contaminants enter groundwater directly from specific sources, such as leaking underground storage tanks, septic systems, or industrial facilities.

2. **Non-Point Source Pollution:** Contaminants infiltrate groundwater indirectly from diffuse sources, such as agricultural runoff, stormwater, and urban runoff.

3. **Landfills and Waste Sites:** Improperly managed landfills and waste disposal sites can release pollutants that migrate into groundwater over time.

4. **Hazardous Materials Spills:** Accidental spills of hazardous materials, chemicals, or fuels can result in groundwater contamination.

Remediation Strategies:

Remediation aims to mitigate and remove contaminants from groundwater, restoring water quality to safe levels. Various strategies can be employed, depending on the nature and extent of contamination:

1. **Natural Attenuation:** Allowing natural processes, such as microbial degradation and dilution, to reduce contaminant concentrations over time.

2. **Pump and Treat:** Extracting contaminated groundwater through pumping wells, treating it above ground, and then re-injecting it into the aquifer or disposing of it properly.

3. **In Situ Bioremediation:** Stimulating naturally occurring microbes to degrade contaminants through nutrient addition, aeration, or other treatments.

4. **Air Sparging:** Injecting air or oxygen into groundwater to enhance the removal of volatile organic compounds.

5. **Chemical Treatment:** Adding chemicals to groundwater to precipitate or neutralize contaminants, making them less mobile or toxic.

6. **Phytoremediation:** Using plants to absorb or break down contaminants through their root systems.

7. **Enhanced Bioremediation:** Introducing specific microbes or nutrients to enhance microbial degradation of contaminants.

8. **Permeable Reactive Barriers:** Installing reactive materials in the subsurface to remove or immobilize contaminants as groundwater flows through.

9. **Ex Situ Treatment:** Pumping contaminated groundwater to the surface for treatment, then re-injecting treated water back into the aquifer.

Site-Specific Approach:

The choice of remediation strategy depends on factors such as the type of contaminants, hydrogeological conditions, and regulatory requirements. Site-specific assessments are crucial to determine the most effective and feasible remediation approach.

Long-Term Monitoring:

Continued monitoring is essential to ensure the success of remediation efforts and verify that contaminant levels remain within acceptable limits.

Addressing groundwater contamination requires a combination of preventative measures, careful site selection, proper borehole construction, and effective remediation techniques. By implementing comprehensive strategies, borehole water systems can provide safe and reliable water resources while safeguarding groundwater quality.

7.3 Mitigating Saltwater Intrusion and Subsidence

Mitigating saltwater intrusion and subsidence is crucial for maintaining the sustainability and functionality of borehole water systems, especially in coastal areas. These phenomena can compromise groundwater quality and availability. Here's how to address saltwater intrusion and subsidence:

Mitigating Saltwater Intrusion:

1. **Aquifer Management:** Establish well-defined extraction zones in coastal aquifers, minimizing withdrawal near the coastline to prevent seawater intrusion.

2. **Freshwater Recharge:** Implement managed aquifer recharge by introducing freshwater into the aquifer during wet periods to create a hydraulic barrier against saltwater intrusion.

3. **Salinity Monitoring:** Regularly monitor groundwater salinity near the coast to detect early signs of intrusion and adjust pumping rates accordingly.

4. **Pumping Limitations:** Enforce pumping limits to ensure that groundwater extraction does not exceed natural recharge rates, preventing excessive drawdown and saltwater intrusion.

5. **Alternative Water Sources:** Explore alternative water sources such as desalination, rainwater harvesting, or treated wastewater for non-potable uses to reduce reliance on groundwater.

6. **Land Use Planning:** Implement land use planning that restricts urban development and industrial activities near coastlines to minimize groundwater demand and contamination risks.

Mitigating Subsidence:

1. **Sustainable Pumping:** Implement pumping rates that are in line with aquifer recharge rates to prevent

excessive groundwater drawdown, which can lead to subsidence.

2. **Aquifer Recharge:** Enhance natural aquifer recharge through strategies such as infiltration basins, retention ponds, and managed recharge programs.

3. **Limit Impervious Surfaces:** Reduce the amount of impermeable surfaces (concrete, asphalt) in urban areas to promote natural groundwater recharge and minimize subsidence risks.

4. **Conservation Measures:** Promote water conservation practices to reduce overall water demand and mitigate the need for excessive groundwater extraction.

5. **Subsidence Monitoring:** Establish subsidence monitoring programs to detect and measure land subsidence early, allowing for timely interventions.

6. **Localized Solutions:** In areas experiencing subsidence, consider localized engineering solutions such as injecting materials (e.g., sand or grout) into the subsurface to counteract compaction.

7. **Community Education:** Educate local communities about the risks of over-pumping, subsidence, and the importance of sustainable groundwater management.

By implementing a combination of management strategies, regulatory measures, and community involvement, borehole water systems can effectively mitigate the risks of saltwater intrusion and subsidence, ensuring the long-term viability of groundwater resources.

8. Socioeconomic and Community Factors

8.1 Socioeconomic Benefits and Challenges

1. **Improved Water Access:** Borehole water systems provide reliable access to clean and safe water, reducing the need for long and arduous journeys to distant water sources.

2. **Health and Hygiene:** Access to clean water contributes to improved health and reduced waterborne diseases, especially among vulnerable populations such as children and the elderly.

3. **Time Savings:** Communities benefit from time saved on water collection, which can be redirected toward

education, income-generating activities, and community development.

4. **Agricultural Productivity:** Borehole water systems support irrigation, enhancing agricultural productivity and food security, leading to increased income and economic stability.

5. **Livelihood Opportunities:** Reliable water supply can enable income-generating activities such as small-scale enterprises, water kiosks, and market gardening.

6. **Education:** Reduced water collection times allow children, particularly girls, to attend school regularly,

leading to improved educational outcomes and future opportunities.

7. **Disaster Resilience:** Borehole water systems can serve as emergency water sources during natural disasters, enhancing community resilience and reducing vulnerability.

Socioeconomic Challenges of Borehole Water Systems:

1. **Cost and Affordability:** The initial investment and ongoing maintenance costs of borehole water systems can be a challenge for communities with limited financial resources.

2. **Equitable Access:** Ensuring equitable access to borehole water can be a challenge, as communities with weaker social structures might face issues of water hoarding or exclusion.

3. **Ownership and Management:** Community ownership and effective management of borehole water systems require strong local governance, technical knowledge, and coordination.

4. **Maintenance and Sustainability:** Sustaining borehole functionality demands regular maintenance, skilled technicians, and adequate funding, which can be difficult to ensure.

5. **Environmental Concerns:** Inadequate management of borehole water systems can lead to overextraction, groundwater depletion, and environmental degradation.

6. **Gender Dynamics:** While borehole water systems can empower women by reducing their water collection burdens, gender disparities in decision-making and resource allocation must be addressed.

7. **Cultural Acceptance:** The introduction of borehole water systems can sometimes disrupt traditional water-sharing practices and relationships within communities.

8. **Water Quality:** Without proper monitoring and treatment, borehole water systems may face water quality challenges, impacting community health.

Addressing these challenges requires a comprehensive approach that includes community engagement, capacity building, sustainable funding models, and integration with broader water resource management strategies. When managed effectively, borehole water systems can contribute significantly to improved socioeconomic conditions and overall community well-being.

8.2 Community Engagement and Participation

Community engagement and participation are essential for the successful implementation, management, and sustainability of borehole water systems. Involving the local community throughout the project lifecycle ensures that their needs, preferences, and knowledge are considered, leading to more effective and impactful outcomes. Here's how community engagement and participation can be integrated into borehole water systems:

Planning and Design Phase:

1. **Needs Assessment:** Conduct thorough assessments to understand the community's water needs, preferences, and cultural practices related to water use.

2. **Community Meetings:** Organize meetings and workshops to gather input from community members, local leaders, and stakeholders to inform the design and location of boreholes.

3. **Cultural Sensitivity:** Respect local traditions, customs, and cultural practices when planning borehole locations and system design.

4. **Ownership and Responsibility:** Empower the community by involving them in decisions about system ownership, management, and operation.

Implementation Phase:

1. **Local Labor and Skills:** Engage community members in construction and installation activities, providing opportunities for employment and skills development.

2. **Training Programs:** Provide training on system maintenance, operation, and water quality monitoring, enabling community members to take ownership of system upkeep.

3. **Community Contributions:** Encourage community contributions, whether financial, in-kind, or labor, to foster a sense of ownership and commitment.

4. **Transparency:** Maintain open communication with the community throughout the implementation process, sharing progress updates and addressing any concerns.

Operation and Management:

1. **Water User Committees:** Establish water user committees comprising community members responsible for overseeing system operation, maintenance, and dispute resolution.

2. **Regular Meetings:** Hold regular community meetings to discuss system performance, address challenges, and make collective decisions.

3. **Revenue Collection:** If applicable, involve the community in setting tariffs and revenue collection mechanisms for system sustainability.

4. **Feedback Mechanisms:** Establish channels for community members to provide feedback, report issues, and suggest improvements related to the borehole water system.

Education and Capacity Building:

1. **Hygiene and Sanitation:** Conduct hygiene and sanitation education programs to raise awareness about proper water use and sanitation practices.

2. **Health Awareness:** Provide education on the importance of clean water for health and encourage water-related hygiene practices.

3. **Sustainability Workshops:** Organize workshops to build community capacity in system maintenance, water conservation, and sustainable water management.

4. **Women's Involvement:** Ensure that women are actively engaged in decision-making processes and that their specific water-related needs are addressed.

Community engagement not only ensures that borehole water systems are tailored to local contexts but also fosters a sense of ownership, responsibility, and pride among community members. By working collaboratively with the community, borehole water systems can contribute to improved livelihoods, health, and overall well-being.

8.3 Equity and Access to Borehole Water Systems

Promoting equity and ensuring equal access to borehole water systems is a fundamental aspect of sustainable and socially responsible water resource management. Addressing issues of equity helps prevent the marginalization of vulnerable groups and ensures that the benefits of borehole water systems are distributed fairly. Here are strategies to promote equity and access:

1. **Inclusive Planning:** Involve diverse community members, including women, elderly individuals, people with disabilities, and marginalized groups, in the planning and decision-making processes related to borehole water systems.

2. **Needs Assessment:** Conduct thorough needs assessments to identify and understand the specific water needs and challenges faced by different community members. Tailor the design and operation of borehole systems to meet these diverse needs.

3. **Accessible Infrastructure:** Design borehole facilities and distribution points with accessibility features to ensure that people with disabilities can use them comfortably. This includes ramps, handrails, and proper signage.

4. **Community Outreach:** Conduct targeted awareness campaigns to ensure that all community members are aware of the borehole water system's benefits, operation, and maintenance requirements.

5. **Equitable Distribution:** Implement fair and transparent mechanisms for water distribution to prevent

hoarding or exclusion. Prioritize vulnerable groups and essential services during water shortages.

6. **Gender Equity:** Empower women by involving them in decision-making processes, water management committees, and capacity-building initiatives related to borehole water systems.

7. **Affordability:** Implement tiered pricing or subsidy programs to ensure that the cost of accessing water remains affordable for all income levels.

8. **Public Participation:** Encourage open dialogue and participation in decision-making, allowing community members to express their needs and concerns.

9. **Local Leadership:** Foster local leadership and community champions who advocate for equitable access and actively engage marginalized groups.

10. **Information Dissemination:** Provide information in multiple formats and languages to ensure that all community members can understand and participate in discussions related to borehole water systems.

11. **Regular Monitoring:** Continuously assess the impacts of the borehole water system on different segments of the community to identify any disparities and take corrective actions.

12. **Capacity Building:** Offer training and capacity-building programs to empower community members, enabling them to take an active role in system management and decision-making.

13. **Conflict Resolution:** Establish mechanisms for resolving conflicts or disputes related to water access, ensuring that they are resolved in a fair and transparent manner.

14. **Long-Term Sustainability:** Develop strategies to ensure that the benefits of borehole water systems are maintained over the long term, preventing future disparities in access.

Promoting equity and access in borehole water systems requires a comprehensive and inclusive approach that respects the rights and needs of all community members. By addressing these considerations, borehole water systems can contribute to improved well-being and social cohesion within communities.

9. Case Studies: Borehole Water Systems in Practice

9.1 Successful Implementation Examples

Several successful examples of borehole water system implementation showcase how communities have benefited from improved water access, sustainability, and overall well-being. Here are a few notable examples:

1. **The PlayPump in South Africa:** PlayPump International introduced a unique borehole system that combined a water pump with a children's merry-go-round. As children played, the pump drew water from the borehole and stored it in a tank. This innovative approach not only provided clean water but also engaged the community, especially children, in maintaining the system.

It demonstrated how creativity can enhance both water access and community involvement.

2. **Solar-Powered Boreholes in Kenya:** Organizations like Water.org and World Vision have implemented solar-powered boreholes in Kenya's rural communities. These boreholes utilize renewable energy to pump water, reducing operational costs and environmental impact. The projects focused on community engagement, training local technicians, and establishing water management committees, leading to improved water sustainability and management.

3. **Boreholes for Disaster Relief in Haiti:** After the 2010 earthquake in Haiti, various NGOs and relief organizations installed borehole water systems to provide immediate and sustainable water access to affected communities. These systems not only addressed urgent water needs but were designed with long-term sustainability and local involvement in mind, contributing to the recovery and rebuilding process.

4. **Community-Managed Boreholes in Uganda:** In Uganda, organizations like WaterAid have supported the establishment of community-managed borehole water systems. These systems involve local communities in decision-making, management, and maintenance. By fostering a sense of ownership and responsibility, these projects have demonstrated improved water quality, equitable access, and reduced downtime due to proactive maintenance.

5. **Integrated Water Management in Bangladesh:**

In Bangladesh, projects led by organizations like BRAC have implemented integrated water management solutions that include borehole water systems, rainwater harvesting, and sanitation facilities. These holistic approaches address multiple water-related challenges and improve overall water security for communities.

6. **Borehole Network in Ethiopia:** The Government of Ethiopia, with support from international organizations, has established a network of borehole water systems to provide reliable water access to rural and remote communities. The project focuses on capacity building, community engagement, and sustainable operation and maintenance practices.

7. **Multi-Use Borehole Systems in Niger:** In Niger, multi-use borehole systems have been implemented, providing water not only for drinking and hygiene but also for agricultural irrigation. These systems contribute to food security, income generation, and improved livelihoods.

These successful examples highlight the importance of community engagement, innovation, sustainable practices, and a comprehensive approach to addressing water challenges through borehole water systems. Each project emphasizes the significance of tailoring solutions to local contexts and involving communities in all stages of implementation and management.

9.2 Lessons Learned from Failed Attempts

Learning from failed attempts at implementing borehole water systems is essential to avoid repeating mistakes and to develop more effective strategies for future projects. Some lessons learned from failed attempts include:

1. **Lack of Community Involvement:** Projects that did not involve the local community in decision-making, planning, and management often faced challenges in sustainability and community ownership.

2. **Inadequate Maintenance:** Borehole water systems that lacked proper maintenance plans and

community capacity-building efforts struggled to address technical issues and maintain functionality.

3. **Limited Technical Expertise:** Projects without sufficient technical expertise for drilling, construction, and system management faced challenges in ensuring proper design, installation, and operation.

4. **Overlooking Socioeconomic Factors:** Ignoring the socioeconomic dynamics of the community, including affordability, gender roles, and cultural norms, led to disconnection between the system and community needs.

5. **Short-Term Focus:** Projects with a short-term focus on immediate water provision rather than long-term

sustainability and maintenance struggled to address ongoing challenges.

6. **Neglecting Water Quality:** Failure to adequately address water quality issues, including contamination and treatment, led to health concerns and reduced community acceptance.

7. **Lack of Monitoring and Evaluation:** Projects that did not establish monitoring and evaluation mechanisms struggled to assess the impact, effectiveness, and ongoing performance of the borehole water systems.

8. **Failure to Address Equity:** Projects that did not address equity issues, such as ensuring access for

vulnerable groups, led to disparities in water availability and utilization.

9. **Unsuitable Technology:** Choosing technology that did not match the hydrogeological conditions, water demand, or energy availability of the area resulted in inefficient systems.

10. **Insufficient Financial Planning:** Projects that did not establish sustainable funding mechanisms for maintenance, repairs, and system upgrades faced challenges in sustaining functionality over time.

11. **Externalization of Decision-Making:** Bypassing local governance structures and making decisions

externally undermined community engagement, local leadership, and ownership.

12. **Lack of Flexibility:** Projects that did not adapt to changing circumstances, such as shifts in water demand or environmental conditions, struggled to remain effective.

13. **Political Instability:** Projects in regions with political instability faced challenges in securing funding, implementing plans, and ensuring community engagement.

14. **Failure to Learn from Previous Failures:** Not learning from past failures and repeating similar mistakes in subsequent projects hindered progress and undermined community trust.

These lessons underscore the importance of a holistic and community-centered approach to borehole water system implementation. By addressing technical, social, financial, and environmental aspects, projects can be better equipped to overcome challenges and contribute to sustainable water access and well-being.

9.3 Case Studies from Different Geographical Regions

Certainly, here are some case studies from different geographical regions showcasing successful borehole water system implementations:

1. **Sub-Saharan Africa: Community-Managed Boreholes in Malawi**

In Malawi, organizations like Water for People have implemented community-managed boreholes. These projects involve local communities in decision-making, maintenance, and operation of the borehole water systems. The approach has led to improved water access, reduced downtime due to proactive maintenance, and increased community ownership.

2. **South Asia: Rainwater Harvesting and Boreholes in India**

In Rajasthan, India, the Jal Bhagirathi Foundation has combined rainwater harvesting and borehole systems to address water scarcity. The project involves community participation, training, and management of boreholes and rainwater storage tanks. This integrated approach has improved water availability for both drinking and agricultural use.

3. **Latin America: Solar-Powered Boreholes in Nicaragua**

In rural Nicaragua, the Solar Electric Light Fund (SELF) has implemented solar-powered boreholes to provide clean water and electricity to remote communities. The solar energy powers the borehole pumps and provides energy for other community needs. This approach has reduced reliance on fossil fuels and improved overall community well-being.

4. **East Asia: Multi-Functional Boreholes in Cambodia**

In Cambodia, the Water and Sanitation Program has implemented multi-functional boreholes that provide not only drinking water but also serve as latrines and composting facilities. This innovative approach addresses water, sanitation, and hygiene needs in an integrated manner, benefiting both health and environment.

5. **Middle East: Desalination Boreholes in Saudi Arabia**

In arid regions like Saudi Arabia, desalination boreholes have been used to address water scarcity. These boreholes tap into brackish or saline aquifers and use desalination techniques to provide potable water. This approach has helped secure water supply in areas with limited freshwater resources.

6. **Oceania: Community-Managed Boreholes in Papua New Guinea**

In rural communities in Papua New Guinea, organizations like WaterAid have supported community-managed borehole projects. These projects involve local engagement, training, and maintenance to ensure sustainable water access. The approach has led to improved health, hygiene, and community cohesion.

These case studies highlight the diverse approaches and innovative solutions used in different regions to implement borehole water systems. Each project emphasizes the importance of community involvement, sustainability, and tailored solutions to address local water challenges.

10. Future Prospects and Recommendations

10.1 Enhancing Regulation and Governance

Enhancing regulation and governance is critical for ensuring the effective and sustainable implementation of borehole water systems. Strong regulatory frameworks and governance structures help address technical, social, environmental, and economic aspects of water resource management. Here's how regulation and governance can be improved:

Regulation:

1. **Legal Frameworks:** Develop and enforce comprehensive legal frameworks that govern borehole

drilling, construction, operation, maintenance, and water quality standards.

2. **Licensing and Permits:** Implement a system for licensing and permitting borehole drilling activities, ensuring that only qualified professionals undertake drilling and construction.

3. **Technical Standards:** Establish clear technical standards for borehole design, construction, and equipment to ensure quality and prevent contamination.

4. **Water Allocation:** Implement water allocation regulations that balance the needs of various water users and prevent overextraction.

5. **Monitoring and Reporting:** Require regular monitoring and reporting of borehole water system performance, water quality, and groundwater levels to ensure compliance with regulations.

6. **Enforcement Mechanisms:** Establish penalties for non-compliance with regulations, and ensure that regulatory agencies have the authority and resources to enforce them effectively.

Governance:

1. **Local Management Committees:** Form water user committees at the community level to oversee borehole water systems, ensuring local ownership and accountability.

2. **Stakeholder Engagement:** Involve local communities, NGOs, academia, and relevant government agencies in decision-making processes and policy development.

3. **Transparency:** Ensure transparency in decision-making, funding allocation, and water allocation to build trust and accountability.

4. **Capacity Building:** Provide training and capacity-building programs for local communities and water management committees to enhance their technical and managerial skills.

5. **Integrated Planning:** Integrate borehole water system planning into broader water resource management strategies, considering the interconnectedness of surface water and groundwater.

6. **Equity and Social Inclusion:** Develop governance structures that prioritize equity, social inclusion, and participation of marginalized groups in decision-making processes.

7. **Data Management:** Establish centralized databases to collect, store, and manage data related to borehole water systems, enabling informed decision-making and policy development.

8. **Conflict Resolution:** Develop mechanisms for resolving conflicts related to water access, distribution, and management through mediation and dialogue.

9. **Long-Term Funding:** Create sustainable funding mechanisms for borehole water system maintenance, repairs, and upgrades through user fees, subsidies, or public-private partnerships.

10. **Adaptive Management:** Continuously review and update regulations and governance structures based on lessons learned, changing conditions, and emerging challenges.

Enhancing regulation and governance ensures that borehole water systems are implemented and managed in a way that benefits communities, protects water resources, and contributes to sustainable development. Effective governance and regulation foster a collaborative approach that involves all stakeholders and promotes the long-term viability of these systems.

10.2 Integrating Borehole Water Systems into Water Management Strategies

Integrating borehole water systems into comprehensive water management strategies enhances their effectiveness, sustainability, and contribution to overall water security. Here's how to effectively integrate borehole water systems into broader water management frameworks:

1. Watershed Management:

- Consider the interaction between borehole water systems and surface water sources within the same watershed.

- Implement measures to protect recharge areas, wetlands, and other natural features that contribute to groundwater replenishment.

2. Aquifer Protection and Recharge:

- Identify and designate areas for aquifer protection and groundwater recharge to maintain groundwater quality and quantity.

- Implement land use practices that minimize contamination risks and promote groundwater recharge.

3. Water Resource Planning:

- Include borehole water systems as a component of regional and national water resource management plans.

- Assess the potential contribution of borehole systems to water supply and demand projections.

4. Drought and Emergency Management:

- Include borehole water systems in drought preparedness and emergency response plans to provide alternative water sources during water shortages.

5. Integrated Water Use Allocation:

- Allocate water resources, including groundwater from borehole systems, based on equitable principles, environmental sustainability, and socioeconomic considerations.

6. Data Sharing and Monitoring:

- Integrate borehole water system data into centralized water monitoring networks to track groundwater levels, quality, and system performance.

7. Technical and Environmental Considerations:

- Ensure that borehole water system development aligns with aquifer characteristics, recharge rates, and the overall groundwater balance.

- Implement sustainable pumping rates to prevent overextraction and maintain aquifer health.

8. Institutional Collaboration:

- Collaborate with relevant government agencies, water utilities, NGOs, and local communities to develop and implement integrated water management plans.

9. Climate Change Resilience:

- Consider the potential impacts of climate change on groundwater availability and incorporate adaptation strategies into water management plans.

10. Social Inclusion and Equity:

- Ensure that water management strategies prioritize equitable access to borehole water systems, especially for vulnerable and marginalized communities.

11. Financing and Investment:

- Allocate funding for borehole water system development, maintenance, and capacity-building within broader water resource budgets.

12. Adaptive Management:

- Continuously review and update water management strategies based on changing hydrological conditions, community needs, and emerging challenges.

Integrating borehole water systems into water management strategies requires a holistic and participatory approach. By considering the interactions between borehole systems and other water sources, aligning policies and regulations, and fostering collaboration among stakeholders, borehole water systems can play a vital role in achieving sustainable and resilient water management at local, regional, and national levels.

10.3 Research Needs and Areas for Further Exploration

Continued research and exploration are essential for advancing our understanding of borehole water systems and optimizing their design, operation, and management. Here are some research needs and areas for further exploration:

1. **Aquifer Characterization:** Conduct detailed hydrogeological studies to understand aquifer properties, recharge rates, and groundwater flow patterns, aiding in sustainable borehole siting and design.

2. **Water Quality Assessment:** Investigate potential contaminants, sources of pollution, and the effectiveness of water treatment methods to ensure safe and potable water from borehole systems.

3. **Climate Change Impact:** Study the potential impacts of climate change on groundwater resources, including changes in recharge patterns, aquifer storage, and water quality.

4. **Sustainability Metrics:** Develop comprehensive indicators and metrics to assess the sustainability of borehole water systems, considering social, economic, environmental, and technical factors.

5. **Innovative Technologies:** Explore new drilling techniques, materials, and pump technologies to enhance borehole construction, efficiency, and durability.

6. **Community Engagement:** Research effective methods for community engagement, participation, and empowerment in borehole water system planning, operation, and management.

7. **Equity and Social Inclusion:** Investigate strategies to ensure equitable access to borehole water systems, especially for marginalized groups, and assess the social impacts of implementation.

8. **Hybrid Systems:** Explore the integration of borehole water systems with other water sources, such as rainwater harvesting, to optimize water supply and promote resilience.

9. **Water-Energy Nexus:** Study the energy requirements of borehole water systems and assess opportunities for renewable energy integration to reduce operational costs and environmental impacts.

10. **Water Rights and Governance:** Examine legal and governance frameworks for equitable water allocation, ownership, and management in the context of borehole systems.

11. **Groundwater Modeling:** Develop accurate groundwater models to simulate borehole system behavior, predict impacts, and optimize pumping rates for sustainable resource management.

12. **Economic Viability:** Analyze the cost-effectiveness of borehole water systems compared to other water supply alternatives, considering both initial investment and long-term operation.

13. **Health Impact Assessment:** Investigate the health impacts of borehole water systems, including waterborne disease reduction, nutrition, and overall community well-being.

14. **Long-Term Monitoring:** Research methodologies and technologies for continuous monitoring of borehole system performance, water quality, and aquifer health.

15. **Decision Support Tools:** Develop tools and models that aid in borehole siting, design, and management, considering various environmental, social, and technical parameters.

16. **Knowledge Sharing and Capacity Building:** Explore effective ways to disseminate best practices, lessons learned, and technical knowledge among practitioners, communities, and policymakers.

By addressing these research needs and areas for further exploration, we can enhance the effectiveness, sustainability, and impact of borehole water systems, contributing to improved water access, resource management, and community well-being.

11. Conclusion

In conclusion, borehole water systems play a pivotal role in addressing water challenges and improving livelihoods around the world. These systems provide reliable and sustainable access to clean and safe water, benefiting communities, agriculture, and various sectors. Through this exploration of "Unlocking the Depths: Exploring the Benefits and Challenges of Borehole Water Systems," we have delved into the multifaceted dimensions of these systems.

We've examined the technical intricacies of borehole construction, aquifer characterization, and water quality assessment. We've explored their socioeconomic significance, ranging from improved health and education to enhanced agriculture and economic opportunities. Equally vital are the challenges and considerations, including equitable access, environmental impacts, and sustainable governance.

Throughout this journey, we've recognized that successful borehole water systems require more than technical expertise; they demand community engagement, stakeholder collaboration, effective regulation, and adaptive management. The integration of borehole water systems into broader water resource strategies underscores their role in enhancing water security, resilience, and sustainable development.

As we navigate a future marked by changing climate patterns, population growth, and evolving water needs, the lessons learned from both successes and failures serve as guiding beacons. By fostering innovation, conducting research, and prioritizing equity, we can unlock the potential of borehole water systems to shape a more water-secure and prosperous world for generations to come.

Appendices:

A. Glossary of Terms

Certainly, here's a glossary of terms related to borehole water systems:

1. **Borehole:** A narrow, deep hole drilled into the ground to access groundwater resources.

2. **Aquifer:** A geological formation that holds water underground, typically consisting of porous rock or sediment that can store and transmit water.

3. **Groundwater:** Water stored below the Earth's surface in aquifers, often accessed through boreholes for various uses.

4. **Recharge:** The process of replenishing groundwater by natural means, such as rainfall or percolation of surface water into the ground.

5. **Drawdown:** The lowering of the water level in a borehole or well due to pumping, indicating the level of groundwater extraction.

6. **Water Table:** The level at which the ground is saturated with water, forming the upper boundary of an unconfined aquifer.

7. **Permeability:** The ability of a material, such as rock or soil, to transmit water or other fluids.

8. **Hydrogeology:** The study of the distribution, movement, and properties of groundwater in the Earth's subsurface.

9. **Water Quality:** The physical, chemical, and biological characteristics of water, including its suitability for specific uses such as drinking, irrigation, and industrial processes.

10. **Recharge Zone:** The area where water infiltrates the ground to replenish an aquifer, often associated with regions of higher elevation.

11. **Pumping Rate:** The volume of water extracted from a borehole or well over a specific time period, typically measured in liters per second or gallons per minute.

12. **Water User Committee:** A group of community members responsible for overseeing the operation, maintenance, and management of a borehole water system.

13. **Desalination:** The process of removing salt and other impurities from seawater or brackish water to make it suitable for drinking and other uses.

14. **Hydraulic Fracturing (Fracking):** A technique used to enhance the permeability of rocks by injecting high-pressure fluid, often water, to create fractures that allow the flow of oil, gas, or water.

15. **Sustainable Development:** Development that meets the needs of the present without compromising the

ability of future generations to meet their own needs, encompassing environmental, social, and economic aspects.

16. **Water Security:** The reliable availability of safe and sufficient water to meet human and ecosystem needs, considering both water quantity and quality.

17. **Equity:** Fair and just distribution of resources, opportunities, and benefits among different groups and communities, considering socioeconomic and cultural factors.

18. **Governance:** The system of rules, institutions, and practices that manage and guide the interactions and

decisions related to a specific domain, such as water management.

19. **Adaptive Management:** A systematic approach that involves continuous learning, monitoring, and adjusting strategies based on changing conditions and new information.

20. **Rainwater Harvesting:** Collecting and storing rainwater for various uses, such as drinking, irrigation, and sanitation.

21. **Community Engagement:** Involving local communities, stakeholders, and beneficiaries in decision-making, planning, and implementation processes.

22. **Resilience:** The ability of a system or community to withstand shocks, adapt to changes, and recover from disturbances while maintaining its functions and structure.

23. **Hygiene and Sanitation:** Practices and behaviors that promote cleanliness, prevent disease transmission, and maintain public health, often related to water use and waste disposal.

This glossary provides definitions for key terms commonly used in the context of borehole water systems and water resource management.

B. List of Acronyms

Certainly, here's a list of acronyms commonly used in discussions related to borehole water systems and water resource management:

1. **NGO:** Non-Governmental Organization

2. **UNICEF:** United Nations Children's Fund

3. **WHO:** World Health Organization

4. **USAID:** United States Agency for International Development

5. **WASH:** Water, Sanitation, and Hygiene

6. **GIS:** Geographic Information System

7. **EIA:** Environmental Impact Assessment

8. **IWRM:** Integrated Water Resource Management

9. **GWP:** Global Water Partnership

10. **SDGs:** Sustainable Development Goals

11. **PPP:** Public-Private Partnership

12. **HDI:** Human Development Index

13. **EFA:** Education for All

14. **FBO:** Faith-Based Organization

15. **GDP:** Gross Domestic Product

16. **NRM:** Natural Resource Management

17. **GIS:** Geographic Information System

18. **CSO:** Civil Society Organization

19. **DWS:** Department of Water and Sanitation

20. **DRC:** Democratic Republic of Congo

21. **LDC:** Least Developed Country

22. **FWR:** Freshwater Resources

23. **LGA:** Local Government Authority

24. **RWH:** Rainwater Harvesting

25. **WUC:** Water User Committee

26. **CRC:** Convention on the Rights of the Child

27. **SACCO:** Savings and Credit Cooperative

28. **ILO:** International Labour Organization

29. **NGP:** National Groundwater Policy

30. **CBO:** Community-Based Organization

These acronyms are commonly used in reports, discussions, and literature related to borehole water systems and water management.

Printed in Great Britain
by Amazon

34672311R00116